家計

Kakeibo

The Art and Science of Saving Money

"You must learn to save first and spend afterwards."

- John Poole

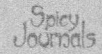

Spicy Journals

Kakeibo Guide
www.spicyjournals.com/kakeibo

Your Plan for the Month

Income for the Month
(projected salary, rental income, royalties, benefits, pension, etc.)

Date	Source	Amount		Date	Source	Amount
Date	Source	Amount		Date	Source	Amount
Date	Source	Amount				

Total Income: ❶

Regular Monthly Outgoings

Rent or Mortgage		Car Insurance	
Utilities (Gas, Electric, Water)		Health Insurance	
Phone		Other Insurance	
Internet		Credit Card Payments	
Cable		Loan Payments	
Memberships		Parking	
Home & Contents Insurance		Commuting (train, bus, petrol...)	
Life Insurance			

Total Outgoings: ❷

Money available:
❶ - ❷

Month:

How much into savings this month?

Your goals for the month:

Your promises to make sure you achieve your goals:

Weekly Spending

	Monday _____	Tuesday _____	Wednesday _____	Thursday _____
Survival (food, medicine, transport, children, etc.)				
Optional (bars, restaurants, takeaway, shopping, etc.)				
Culture (books, music, shows, movies, magazines, education)				
Extra (irregular things such as gifts, repairs, furniture, unexpected expenses etc.)				

Month:			**Week 1**
Friday _____	Saturday _____	Sunday _____	**Total**
			Survival
			Optional
			Culture
			Extra

Weekly Spending

	Monday _____	Tuesday _____	Wednesday _____	Thursday _____
Survival (food, medicine, transport, children, etc.)				
Optional (bars, restaurants, takeaway, shopping, etc.)				
Culture (books, music, shows, movies, magazines, education)				
Extra (irregular things such as gifts, repairs, furniture, unexpected expenses etc.)				

Month: [　　　　　　] Week 2

Friday _____	Saturday _____	Sunday _____	Total	
				Survival
				Optional
				Culture
				Extra

Weekly Spending

	Monday _____	Tuesday _____	Wednesday _____	Thursday _____
Survival (food, medicine, transport, children, etc.)				
Optional (bars, restaurants, takeaway, shopping, etc.)				
Culture (books, music, shows, movies, magazines, education)				
Extra (irregular things such as gifts, repairs, furniture, unexpected expenses etc.)				

Month: [ ]

Week 3

Friday _____	Saturday _____	Sunday _____	Total	
				Survival
				Optional
				Culture
				Extra

Weekly Spending

	Monday	Tuesday	Wednesday	Thursday
Survival (food, medicine, transport, children, etc.)				
Optional (bars, restaurants, takeaway, shopping, etc.)				
Culture (books, music, shows, movies, magazines, education)				
Extra (irregular things such as gifts, repairs, furniture, unexpected expenses etc.)				

Month: [ ]   Week 4

Friday ____	Saturday ____	Sunday ____	Total	
				Survival
				Optional
				Culture
				Extra

Weekly Spending

	Monday _____	Tuesday _____	Wednesday _____	Thursday _____
Survival (food, medicine, transport, children, etc.)				
Optional (bars, restaurants, takeaway, shopping, etc.)				
Culture (books, music, shows, movies, magazines, education)				
Extra (irregular things such as gifts, repairs, furniture, unexpected expenses etc.)				

Month: [ ] Week 5

Friday _____	Saturday _____	Sunday _____	Total	
				Survival
				Optional
				Culture
				Extra

Review of the Month

Your spending by category

	Survival	Optional	Culture	Extra
Week 1				
Week 2				
Week 3				
Week 4				
Week 5				
Total				

Your savings this month

Your total outgoings for the month:	
How much did you have to spend? ❶ - ❷	
How much did you decide to save?	
How much did you actually save?	

Did you achieve your goal for savings? ☐ Yes ☐ No ☐ So close

Month:

Reflections on the month in seven words or less:

If only...

What will you do to improve next month?

Your Plan for the Month

Income for the Month
(projected salary, rental income, royalties, benefits, pension, etc.)

Date	Source	Amount	Date	Source	Amount
Date	Source	Amount	Date	Source	Amount
Date	Source	Amount			

Total Income: ❶

Regular Monthly Outgoings

Rent or Mortgage		Car Insurance			
Utilities (Gas, Electric, Water)		Health Insurance			
Phone		Other Insurance			
Internet		Credit Card Payments			
Cable		Loan Payments			
Memberships		Parking			
Home & Contents Insurance		Commuting (train, bus, petrol...)			
Life Insurance					

Total Outgoings: ❷

Money available:
❶ - ❷

Month:

How much into savings this month?

Your goals for the month:

Your promises to make sure you achieve your goals:

Weekly Spending

	Monday _____	Tuesday _____	Wednesday _____	Thursday _____
Survival (food, medicine, transport, children, etc.)				
Optional (bars, restaurants, takeaway, shopping, etc.)				
Culture (books, music, shows, movies, magazines, education)				
Extra (irregular things such as gifts, repairs, furniture, unexpected expenses etc.)				

Month: [   ]   Week 1

Friday _____	Saturday _____	Sunday _____	Total	
				Survival
				Optional
				Culture
				Extra

Weekly Spending

	Monday	Tuesday	Wednesday	Thursday
Survival (food, medicine, transport, children, etc.)				
Optional (bars, restaurants, takeaway, shopping, etc.)				
Culture (books, music, shows, movies, magazines, education)				
Extra (irregular things such as gifts, repairs, furniture, unexpected expenses etc.)				

Month:

Week 2

Friday _____	Saturday _____	Sunday _____	Total	
				Survival
				Optional
				Culture
				Extra

Weekly Spending

	Monday _____	Tuesday _____	Wednesday _____	Thursday _____
Survival (food, medicine, transport, children, etc.)				
Optional (bars, restaurants, takeaway, shopping, etc.)				
Culture (books, music, shows, movies, magazines, education)				
Extra (irregular things such as gifts, repairs, furniture, unexpected expenses etc.)				

Month:　　　　　　　　　　　　Week 3

Friday	Saturday	Sunday	Total	
				Survival
				Optional
				Culture
				Extra

Weekly Spending

	Monday _____	Tuesday _____	Wednesday _____	Thursday _____
Survival (food, medicine, transport, children, etc.)				
Optional (bars, restaurants, takeaway, shopping, etc.)				
Culture (books, music, shows, movies, magazines, education)				
Extra (irregular things such as gifts, repairs, furniture, unexpected expenses etc.)				

Month: ☐   Week 4

Friday ____	Saturday ____	Sunday ____	Total
			Survival
			Optional
			Culture
			Extra

Weekly Spending

	Monday _____	Tuesday _____	Wednesday _____	Thursday _____
Survival (food, medicine, transport, children, etc.)				
Optional (bars, restaurants, takeaway, shopping, etc.)				
Culture (books, music, shows, movies, magazines, education)				
Extra (irregular things such as gifts, repairs, furniture, unexpected expenses etc.)				

Month: _____   Week 5

Friday _____	Saturday _____	Sunday _____	Total	
				Survival
				Optional
				Culture
				Extra

Review of the Month

Your spending by category

	Survival	Optional	Culture	Extra
Week 1				
Week 2				
Week 3				
Week 4				
Week 5				
Total				

Your savings this month

Your total outgoings for the month:	
How much did you have to spend? ❶ - ❷	
How much did you decide to save?	
How much did you actually save?	

Did you achieve your goal for savings?   ☐ Yes   ☐ No   ☐ So close

Month:

Reflections on the month in seven words or less:

If only...

What will you do to improve next month?

Your Plan for the Month

Income for the Month
(projected salary, rental income, royalties, benefits, pension, etc.)

Date	Source	Amount	Date	Source	Amount
Date	Source	Amount	Date	Source	Amount
Date	Source	Amount			

Total Income: ❶

Regular Monthly Outgoings

Rent or Mortgage		Car Insurance			
Utilities (Gas, Electric, Water)		Health Insurance			
Phone		Other Insurance			
Internet		Credit Card Payments			
Cable		Loan Payments			
Memberships		Parking			
Home & Contents Insurance		Commuting (train, bus, petrol...)			
Life Insurance					

Total Outgoings: ❷

Money available: ❶ - ❷ ☐

Month: ☐

How much into savings this month? ☐

Your goals for the month:

Your promises to make sure you achieve your goals:

Weekly Spending

	Monday _____	Tuesday _____	Wednesday _____	Thursday _____
Survival (food, medicine, transport, children, etc.)				
Optional (bars, restaurants, takeaway, shopping, etc.)				
Culture (books, music, shows, movies, magazines, education)				
Extra (irregular things such as gifts, repairs, furniture, unexpected expenses etc.)				

Month: [ ] Week 1

Friday _____	Saturday _____	Sunday _____	Total	
				Survival
				Optional
				Culture
				Extra

Weekly Spending

	Monday _____	Tuesday _____	Wednesday _____	Thursday _____
Survival (food, medicine, transport, children, etc.)				
Optional (bars, restaurants, takeaway, shopping, etc.)				
Culture (books, music, shows, movies, magazines, education)				
Extra (irregular things such as gifts, repairs, furniture, unexpected expenses etc.)				

Month:

Week 2

Friday _____	Saturday _____	Sunday _____	Total	
				Survival
				Optional
				Culture
				Extra

Weekly Spending

	Monday _____	Tuesday _____	Wednesday _____	Thursday _____
Survival (food, medicine, transport, children, etc.)				
Optional (bars, restaurants, takeaway, shopping, etc.)				
Culture (books, music, shows, movies, magazines, education)				
Extra (irregular things such as gifts, repairs, furniture, unexpected expenses etc.)				

Month: [   ]   Week 3

Friday _____	Saturday _____	Sunday _____	Total	
				Survival
				Optional
				Culture
				Extra

37

Weekly Spending

	Monday _____	Tuesday _____	Wednesday _____	Thursday _____
Survival (food, medicine, transport, children, etc.)				
Optional (bars, restaurants, takeaway, shopping, etc.)				
Culture (books, music, shows, movies, magazines, education)				
Extra (irregular things such as gifts, repairs, furniture, unexpected expenses etc.)				

Month: ☐   Week 4

Friday ____	Saturday ____	Sunday ____	Total	
				Survival
				Optional
				Culture
				Extra

Weekly Spending

	Monday	Tuesday	Wednesday	Thursday
Survival (food, medicine, transport, children, etc.)				
Optional (bars, restaurants, takeaway, shopping, etc.)				
Culture (books, music, shows, movies, magazines, education)				
Extra (irregular things such as gifts, repairs, furniture, unexpected expenses etc.)				

Month: [   ]   Week 5

Friday _____	Saturday _____	Sunday _____	Total	
				Survival
				Optional
				Culture
				Extra

Review of the Month

Your spending by category

	Survival	Optional	Culture	Extra
Week 1				
Week 2				
Week 3				
Week 4				
Week 5				
Total				

Your savings this month

Your total outgoings for the month:	
How much did you have to spend? ❶ - ❷	
How much did you decide to save?	
How much did you actually save?	

Did you achieve your goal for savings? ☐ Yes ☐ No ☐ So close

Month:

Reflections on the month in seven words or less:

If only...

What will you do to improve next month?

Your Plan for the Month

Income for the Month
(projected salary, rental income, royalties, benefits, pension, etc.)

Date	Source	Amount	Date	Source	Amount
Date	Source	Amount	Date	Source	Amount
Date	Source	Amount			

Total Income: ❶

Regular Monthly Outgoings

Rent or Mortgage		Car Insurance			
Utilities (Gas, Electric, Water)		Health Insurance			
Phone		Other Insurance			
Internet		Credit Card Payments			
Cable		Loan Payments			
Memberships		Parking			
Home & Contents Insurance		Commuting (train, bus, petrol...)			
Life Insurance					

Total Outgoings: ❷

Money available:
❶ - ❷

Month:

How much into savings this month?

Your goals for the month:

Your promises to make sure you achieve your goals:

Weekly Spending

	Monday _____	Tuesday _____	Wednesday _____	Thursday _____
Survival (food, medicine, transport, children, etc.)				
Optional (bars, restaurants, takeaway, shopping, etc.)				
Culture (books, music, shows, movies, magazines, education)				
Extra (irregular things such as gifts, repairs, furniture, unexpected expenses etc.)				

Month: [   ]   Week 1

Friday _____	Saturday _____	Sunday _____	Total	
				Survival
				Optional
				Culture
				Extra

Weekly Spending

	Monday _____	Tuesday _____	Wednesday _____	Thursday _____
Survival (food, medicine, transport, children, etc.)				
Optional (bars, restaurants, takeaway, shopping, etc.)				
Culture (books, music, shows, movies, magazines, education)				
Extra (irregular things such as gifts, repairs, furniture, unexpected expenses etc.)				

Month: [ ] Week 2

Friday ____	Saturday ____	Sunday ____	Total	
				Survival
				Optional
				Culture
				Extra

Weekly Spending

	Monday _____	Tuesday _____	Wednesday _____	Thursday _____
Survival (food, medicine, transport, children, etc.)				
Optional (bars, restaurants, takeaway, shopping, etc.)				
Culture (books, music, shows, movies, magazines, education)				
Extra (irregular things such as gifts, repairs, furniture, unexpected expenses etc.)				

Month: _____   Week 3

Friday _____	Saturday _____	Sunday _____	Total	
				Survival
				Optional
				Culture
				Extra

Weekly Spending

	Monday _____	Tuesday _____	Wednesday _____	Thursday _____
Survival (food, medicine, transport, children, etc.)				
Optional (bars, restaurants, takeaway, shopping, etc.)				
Culture (books, music, shows, movies, magazines, education)				
Extra (irregular things such as gifts, repairs, furniture, unexpected expenses etc.)				

Month: [   ]   Week 4

Friday _____	Saturday _____	Sunday _____	Total	
				Survival
				Optional
				Culture
				Extra

Weekly Spending

	Monday _____	Tuesday _____	Wednesday _____	Thursday _____
Survival (food, medicine, transport, children, etc.)				
Optional (bars, restaurants, takeaway, shopping, etc.)				
Culture (books, music, shows, movies, magazines, education)				
Extra (irregular things such as gifts, repairs, furniture, unexpected expenses etc.)				

Month:

Week 5

Friday _____	Saturday _____	Sunday _____	Total	
				Survival
				Optional
				Culture
				Extra

55

Review of the Month

Your spending by category

	Survival	Optional	Culture	Extra
Week 1				
Week 2				
Week 3				
Week 4				
Week 5				
Total				

Your savings this month

Your total outgoings for the month:	
How much did you have to spend? ❶ - ❷	
How much did you decide to save?	
How much did you actually save?	

Did you achieve your goal for savings? ☐ Yes   ☐ No   ☐ So close

Month:

Reflections on the month in seven words or less:

If only...

What will you do to improve next month?

Your Plan for the Month

Income for the Month
(projected salary, rental income, royalties, benefits, pension, etc.)

Date	Source	Amount	Date	Source	Amount
Date	Source	Amount	Date	Source	Amount
Date	Source	Amount			

Total Income: ❶

Regular Monthly Outgoings

Rent or Mortgage		Car Insurance			
Utilities (Gas, Electric, Water)		Health Insurance			
Phone		Other Insurance			
Internet		Credit Card Payments			
Cable		Loan Payments			
Memberships		Parking			
Home & Contents Insurance		Commuting (train, bus, petrol...)			
Life Insurance					

Total Outgoings: ❷

Money available:
❶ - ❷

Month:

How much into savings this month?

Your goals for the month:

Your promises to make sure you achieve your goals:

Weekly Spending

	Monday _____	Tuesday _____	Wednesday _____	Thursday _____
Survival (food, medicine, transport, children, etc.)				
Optional (bars, restaurants, takeaway, shopping, etc.)				
Culture (books, music, shows, movies, magazines, education)				
Extra (irregular things such as gifts, repairs, furniture, unexpected expenses etc.)				

Month: _____ Week 1

Friday _____	Saturday _____	Sunday _____	Total	
				Survival
				Optional
				Culture
				Extra

Weekly Spending

	Monday	Tuesday	Wednesday	Thursday
Survival (food, medicine, transport, children, etc.)				
Optional (bars, restaurants, takeaway, shopping, etc.)				
Culture (books, music, shows, movies, magazines, education)				
Extra (irregular things such as gifts, repairs, furniture, unexpected expenses etc.)				

Month: _____   **Week 2**

Friday _____	Saturday _____	Sunday _____	Total	
				Survival
				Optional
				Culture
				Extra

Weekly Spending

	Monday _____	Tuesday _____	Wednesday _____	Thursday _____
Survival (food, medicine, transport, children, etc.)				
Optional (bars, restaurants, takeaway, shopping, etc.)				
Culture (books, music, shows, movies, magazines, education)				
Extra (irregular things such as gifts, repairs, furniture, unexpected expenses etc.)				

Month:

Week 3

Friday _____	Saturday _____	Sunday _____	Total	
				Survival
				Optional
				Culture
				Extra

Weekly Spending

	Monday	Tuesday	Wednesday	Thursday
Survival (food, medicine, transport, children, etc.)				
Optional (bars, restaurants, takeaway, shopping, etc.)				
Culture (books, music, shows, movies, magazines, education)				
Extra (irregular things such as gifts, repairs, furniture, unexpected expenses etc.)				

Month:

Week 4

Friday _____	Saturday _____	Sunday _____	Total	
				Survival
				Optional
				Culture
				Extra

Weekly Spending

	Monday	Tuesday	Wednesday	Thursday
Survival (food, medicine, transport, children, etc.)				
Optional (bars, restaurants, takeaway, shopping, etc.)				
Culture (books, music, shows, movies, magazines, education)				
Extra (irregular things such as gifts, repairs, furniture, unexpected expenses etc.)				

Month: ☐   **Week 5**

Friday ____	Saturday ____	Sunday ____	Total	
				Survival
				Optional
				Culture
				Extra

Review of the Month

Your spending by category

	Survival	Optional	Culture	Extra
Week 1				
Week 2				
Week 3				
Week 4				
Week 5				
Total				

Your savings this month

Your total outgoings for the month:	
How much did you have to spend? ❶ − ❷	
How much did you decide to save?	
How much did you actually save?	

Did you achieve your goal for savings? ☐ Yes ☐ No ☐ So close

Month:

Reflections on the month in seven words or less:

If only...

What will you do to improve next month?

Your Plan for the Month

Income for the Month
(projected salary, rental income, royalties, benefits, pension, etc.)

Date	Source	Amount	Date	Source	Amount
Date	Source	Amount	Date	Source	Amount
Date	Source	Amount			

Total Income: ❶

Regular Monthly Outgoings

Rent or Mortgage		Car Insurance			
Utilities (Gas, Electric, Water)		Health Insurance			
Phone		Other Insurance			
Internet		Credit Card Payments			
Cable		Loan Payments			
Memberships		Parking			
Home & Contents Insurance		Commuting (train, bus, petrol...)			
Life Insurance					

Total Outgoings: ❷

Money available:
❶ - ❷

Month:

How much into savings this month?

Your goals for the month:

Your promises to make sure you achieve your goals:

Weekly Spending

	Monday _____	Tuesday _____	Wednesday _____	Thursday _____
Survival (food, medicine, transport, children, etc.)				
Optional (bars, restaurants, takeaway, shopping, etc.)				
Culture (books, music, shows, movies, magazines, education)				
Extra (irregular things such as gifts, repairs, furniture, unexpected expenses etc.)				

Month: _____   **Week 1**

Friday _____	Saturday _____	Sunday _____	**Total**	
				Survival
				Optional
				Culture
				Extra

Weekly Spending

	Monday _____	Tuesday _____	Wednesday _____	Thursday _____
Survival (food, medicine, transport, children, etc.)				
Optional (bars, restaurants, takeaway, shopping, etc.)				
Culture (books, music, shows, movies, magazines, education)				
Extra (irregular things such as gifts, repairs, furniture, unexpected expenses etc.)				

Month: ☐   Week 2

Friday ____	Saturday ____	Sunday ____	Total
			Survival
			Optional
			Culture
			Extra

Weekly Spending

	Monday _____	Tuesday _____	Wednesday _____	Thursday _____
Survival (food, medicine, transport, children, etc.)				
Optional (bars, restaurants, takeaway, shopping, etc.)				
Culture (books, music, shows, movies, magazines, education)				
Extra (irregular things such as gifts, repairs, furniture, unexpected expenses etc.)				

Month: _____   Week 3

Friday _____	Saturday _____	Sunday _____	Total	
				Survival
				Optional
				Culture
				Extra

79

Weekly Spending

	Monday _____	Tuesday _____	Wednesday _____	Thursday _____
Survival (food, medicine, transport, children, etc.)				
Optional (bars, restaurants, takeaway, shopping, etc.)				
Culture (books, music, shows, movies, magazines, education)				
Extra (irregular things such as gifts, repairs, furniture, unexpected expenses etc.)				

Month: _____   **Week 4**

Friday _____	Saturday _____	Sunday _____	Total	
				Survival
				Optional
				Culture
				Extra

Weekly Spending

	Monday _____	Tuesday _____	Wednesday _____	Thursday _____
Survival (food, medicine, transport, children, etc.)				
Optional (bars, restaurants, takeaway, shopping, etc.)				
Culture (books, music, shows, movies, magazines, education)				
Extra (irregular things such as gifts, repairs, furniture, unexpected expenses etc.)				

Month: _____   Week 5

Friday _____	Saturday _____	Sunday _____	Total
			Survival
			Optional
			Culture
			Extra

Review of the Month

Your spending by category

	Survival	Optional	Culture	Extra
Week 1				
Week 2				
Week 3				
Week 4				
Week 5				
Total				

Your savings this month

Your total outgoings for the month:	
How much did you have to spend? ❶ - ❷	
How much did you decide to save?	
How much did you actually save?	

Did you achieve your goal for savings? ☐ Yes ☐ No ☐ So close

Month:

Reflections on the month in seven words or less:

If only...

What will you do to improve next month?

Your Plan for the Month

Income for the Month
(projected salary, rental income, royalties, benefits, pension, etc.)

Date	Source	Amount	Date	Source	Amount
Date	Source	Amount	Date	Source	Amount
Date	Source	Amount	**Total Income:** ❶		

Regular Monthly Outgoings

Rent or Mortgage		Car Insurance		
Utilities (Gas, Electric, Water)		Health Insurance		
Phone		Other Insurance		
Internet		Credit Card Payments		
Cable		Loan Payments		
Memberships		Parking		
Home & Contents Insurance		Commuting (train, bus, petrol...)		
Life Insurance		**Total Outgoings:** ❷		

Money available: ❶ - ❷

Month:

How much into savings this month?

Your goals for the month:

Your promises to make sure you achieve your goals:

Weekly Spending

	Monday _____	Tuesday _____	Wednesday _____	Thursday _____
Survival (food, medicine, transport, children, etc.)				
Optional (bars, restaurants, takeaway, shopping, etc.)				
Culture (books, music, shows, movies, magazines, education)				
Extra (irregular things such as gifts, repairs, furniture, unexpected expenses etc.)				

Month: [_____]   Week 1

Friday _____	Saturday _____	Sunday _____	Total	
				Survival
				Optional
				Culture
				Extra

Weekly Spending

	Monday _____	Tuesday _____	Wednesday _____	Thursday _____
Survival (food, medicine, transport, children, etc.)				
Optional (bars, restaurants, takeaway, shopping, etc.)				
Culture (books, music, shows, movies, magazines, education)				
Extra (irregular things such as gifts, repairs, furniture, unexpected expenses etc.)				

Month:

Week 2

Friday _____	Saturday _____	Sunday _____	Total	
				Survival
				Optional
				Culture
				Extra

Weekly Spending

	Monday _____	Tuesday _____	Wednesday _____	Thursday _____
Survival (food, medicine, transport, children, etc.)				
Optional (bars, restaurants, takeaway, shopping, etc.)				
Culture (books, music, shows, movies, magazines, education)				
Extra (irregular things such as gifts, repairs, furniture, unexpected expenses etc.)				

Month: ☐   **Week 3**

Friday ___	Saturday ___	Sunday ___	**Total**	
				Survival
				Optional
				Culture
				Extra

93

Weekly Spending

	Monday _____	Tuesday _____	Wednesday _____	Thursday _____
Survival (food, medicine, transport, children, etc.)				
Optional (bars, restaurants, takeaway, shopping, etc.)				
Culture (books, music, shows, movies, magazines, education)				
Extra (irregular things such as gifts, repairs, furniture, unexpected expenses etc.)				

Month: [   ] Week 4

Friday _____	Saturday _____	Sunday _____	Total	
				Survival
				Optional
				Culture
				Extra

Weekly Spending

	Monday _____	Tuesday _____	Wednesday _____	Thursday _____
Survival (food, medicine, transport, children, etc.)				
Optional (bars, restaurants, takeaway, shopping, etc.)				
Culture (books, music, shows, movies, magazines, education)				
Extra (irregular things such as gifts, repairs, furniture, unexpected expenses etc.)				

Month: [   ]   Week 5

Friday _____	Saturday _____	Sunday _____	Total	
				Survival
				Optional
				Culture
				Extra

Review of the Month

Your spending by category

	Survival	Optional	Culture	Extra
Week 1				
Week 2				
Week 3				
Week 4				
Week 5				
Total				

Your savings this month

Your total outgoings for the month:	
How much did you have to spend? ❶ - ❷	
How much did you decide to save?	
How much did you actually save?	

Did you achieve your goal for savings?   ☐ Yes   ☐ No   ☐ So close

Month:

Reflections on the month in seven words or less:

If only...

What will you do to improve next month?

Your Plan for the Month

Income for the Month
(projected salary, rental income, royalties, benefits, pension, etc.)

Date	Source	Amount	Date	Source	Amount
Date	Source	Amount	Date	Source	Amount
Date	Source	Amount			

Total Income: ❶

Regular Monthly Outgoings

Rent or Mortgage		Car Insurance			
Utilities (Gas, Electric, Water)		Health Insurance			
Phone		Other Insurance			
Internet		Credit Card Payments			
Cable		Loan Payments			
Memberships		Parking			
Home & Contents Insurance		Commuting (train, bus, petrol...)			
Life Insurance					

Total Outgoings: ❷

Money available:
❶ - ❷

Month:

How much into savings this month?

Your goals for the month:

Your promises to make sure you achieve your goals:

Weekly Spending

	Monday _____	Tuesday _____	Wednesday _____	Thursday _____
Survival (food, medicine, transport, children, etc.)				
Optional (bars, restaurants, takeaway, shopping, etc.)				
Culture (books, music, shows, movies, magazines, education)				
Extra (irregular things such as gifts, repairs, furniture, unexpected expenses etc.)				

Month: _____   Week 1

Friday _____	Saturday _____	Sunday _____	Total	
				Survival
				Optional
				Culture
				Extra

Weekly Spending

	Monday _____	Tuesday _____	Wednesday _____	Thursday _____
Survival (food, medicine, transport, children, etc.)				
Optional (bars, restaurants, takeaway, shopping, etc.)				
Culture (books, music, shows, movies, magazines, education)				
Extra (irregular things such as gifts, repairs, furniture, unexpected expenses etc.)				

Month: _____   Week 2

Friday _____	Saturday _____	Sunday _____	Total	
				Survival
				Optional
				Culture
				Extra

Weekly Spending

	Monday _____	Tuesday _____	Wednesday _____	Thursday _____
Survival (food, medicine, transport, children, etc.)				
Optional (bars, restaurants, takeaway, shopping, etc.)				
Culture (books, music, shows, movies, magazines, education)				
Extra (irregular things such as gifts, repairs, furniture, unexpected expenses etc.)				

Month:

Week 3

Friday _____	Saturday _____	Sunday _____	Total	
				Survival
				Optional
				Culture
				Extra

Weekly Spending

	Monday _____	Tuesday _____	Wednesday _____	Thursday _____
Survival (food, medicine, transport, children, etc.)				
Optional (bars, restaurants, takeaway, shopping, etc.)				
Culture (books, music, shows, movies, magazines, education)				
Extra (irregular things such as gifts, repairs, furniture, unexpected expenses etc.)				

Month:		Week 4

Friday _____	Saturday _____	Sunday _____	Total	
				Survival
				Optional
				Culture
				Extra

Weekly Spending

	Monday _____	Tuesday _____	Wednesday _____	Thursday _____
Survival (food, medicine, transport, children, etc.)				
Optional (bars, restaurants, takeaway, shopping, etc.)				
Culture (books, music, shows, movies, magazines, education)				
Extra (irregular things such as gifts, repairs, furniture, unexpected expenses etc.)				

Month: ☐   **Week 5**

Friday _____	Saturday _____	Sunday _____	Total	
				Survival
				Optional
				Culture
				Extra

Review of the Month

Your spending by category

	Survival	Optional	Culture	Extra
Week 1				
Week 2				
Week 3				
Week 4				
Week 5				
Total				

Your savings this month

Your total outgoings for the month:	
How much did you have to spend? ❶ - ❷	
How much did you decide to save?	
How much did you actually save?	

Did you achieve your goal for savings?   ☐ Yes   ☐ No   ☐ So close

Month:

Reflections on the month in seven words or less:

If only...

What will you do to improve next month?

Your Plan for the Month

Income for the Month
(projected salary, rental income, royalties, benefits, pension, etc.)

Date	Source	Amount	Date	Source	Amount
Date	Source	Amount	Date	Source	Amount
Date	Source	Amount			

Total Income: ❶

Regular Monthly Outgoings

Rent or Mortgage		Car Insurance	
Utilities (Gas, Electric, Water)		Health Insurance	
Phone		Other Insurance	
Internet		Credit Card Payments	
Cable		Loan Payments	
Memberships		Parking	
Home & Contents Insurance		Commuting (train, bus, petrol...)	
Life Insurance			

Total Outgoings: ❷

Money available:
❶ - ❷

Month:

How much into savings this month?

Your goals for the month:

Your promises to make sure you achieve your goals:

Weekly Spending

	Monday _____	Tuesday _____	Wednesday _____	Thursday _____
Survival (food, medicine, transport, children, etc.)				
Optional (bars, restaurants, takeaway, shopping, etc.)				
Culture (books, music, shows, movies, magazines, education)				
Extra (irregular things such as gifts, repairs, furniture, unexpected expenses etc.)				

Month: _____   Week 1

Friday _____	Saturday _____	Sunday _____	Total	
				Survival
				Optional
				Culture
				Extra

Weekly Spending

	Monday _____	Tuesday _____	Wednesday _____	Thursday _____
Survival (food, medicine, transport, children, etc.)				
Optional (bars, restaurants, takeaway, shopping, etc.)				
Culture (books, music, shows, movies, magazines, education)				
Extra (irregular things such as gifts, repairs, furniture, unexpected expenses etc.)				

Month: | Week 2

Friday	Saturday	Sunday	Total	
				Survival
				Optional
				Culture
				Extra

Weekly Spending

	Monday _____	Tuesday _____	Wednesday _____	Thursday _____
Survival (food, medicine, transport, children, etc.)				
Optional (bars, restaurants, takeaway, shopping, etc.)				
Culture (books, music, shows, movies, magazines, education)				
Extra (irregular things such as gifts, repairs, furniture, unexpected expenses etc.)				

Month: _____ Week 3

Friday _____	Saturday _____	Sunday _____	Total	
				Survival
				Optional
				Culture
				Extra

Weekly Spending

	Monday _____	Tuesday _____	Wednesday _____	Thursday _____
Survival (food, medicine, transport, children, etc.)				
Optional (bars, restaurants, takeaway, shopping, etc.)				
Culture (books, music, shows, movies, magazines, education)				
Extra (irregular things such as gifts, repairs, furniture, unexpected expenses etc.)				

Month:

Week 4

Friday _____	Saturday _____	Sunday _____	Total
			Survival
			Optional
			Culture
			Extra

Weekly Spending

	Monday _____	Tuesday _____	Wednesday _____	Thursday _____
Survival (food, medicine, transport, children, etc.)				
Optional (bars, restaurants, takeaway, shopping, etc.)				
Culture (books, music, shows, movies, magazines, education)				
Extra (irregular things such as gifts, repairs, furniture, unexpected expenses etc.)				

Month: _____   Week 5

Friday _____	Saturday _____	Sunday _____	Total	
				Survival
				Optional
				Culture
				Extra

Review of the Month

Your spending by category

	Survival	Optional	Culture	Extra
Week 1				
Week 2				
Week 3				
Week 4				
Week 5				
Total				

Your savings this month

Your total outgoings for the month:	
How much did you have to spend? ❶ - ❷	
How much did you decide to save?	
How much did you actually save?	

Did you achieve your goal for savings? ☐ Yes ☐ No ☐ So close

Month:

Reflections on the month in seven words or less:

If only...

What will you do to improve next month?

Your Plan for the Month

Income for the Month
(projected salary, rental income, royalties, benefits, pension, etc.)

Date	Source	Amount	Date	Source	Amount
Date	Source	Amount	Date	Source	Amount
Date	Source	Amount			

Total Income: ❶

Regular Monthly Outgoings

Rent or Mortgage		Car Insurance	
Utilities (Gas, Electric, Water)		Health Insurance	
Phone		Other Insurance	
Internet		Credit Card Payments	
Cable		Loan Payments	
Memberships		Parking	
Home & Contents Insurance		Commuting (train, bus, petrol...)	
Life Insurance			

Total Outgoings: ❷

Money available:
❶ - ❷

Month:

How much into savings this month?

Your goals for the month:

Your promises to make sure you achieve your goals:

Weekly Spending

	Monday	Tuesday	Wednesday	Thursday
Survival (food, medicine, transport, children, etc.)				
Optional (bars, restaurants, takeaway, shopping, etc.)				
Culture (books, music, shows, movies, magazines, education)				
Extra (irregular things such as gifts, repairs, furniture, unexpected expenses etc.)				

Month: [　　　　　　　　] Week 1

Friday _____	Saturday _____	Sunday _____	Total	
				Survival
				Optional
				Culture
				Extra

Weekly Spending

	Monday _____	Tuesday _____	Wednesday _____	Thursday _____
Survival (food, medicine, transport, children, etc.)				
Optional (bars, restaurants, takeaway, shopping, etc.)				
Culture (books, music, shows, movies, magazines, education)				
Extra (irregular things such as gifts, repairs, furniture, unexpected expenses etc.)				

Month:

Week 2

Friday _____	Saturday _____	Sunday _____	Total	
				Survival
				Optional
				Culture
				Extra

133

Weekly Spending

	Monday _____	Tuesday _____	Wednesday _____	Thursday _____
Survival (food, medicine, transport, children, etc.)				
Optional (bars, restaurants, takeaway, shopping, etc.)				
Culture (books, music, shows, movies, magazines, education)				
Extra (irregular things such as gifts, repairs, furniture, unexpected expenses etc.)				

Month:

Week 3

Friday _____	Saturday _____	Sunday _____	Total	
				Survival
				Optional
				Culture
				Extra

Weekly Spending

	Monday _____	Tuesday _____	Wednesday _____	Thursday _____
Survival (food, medicine, transport, children, etc.)				
Optional (bars, restaurants, takeaway, shopping, etc.)				
Culture (books, music, shows, movies, magazines, education)				
Extra (irregular things such as gifts, repairs, furniture, unexpected expenses etc.)				

Month:

Week 4

Friday _____	Saturday _____	Sunday _____	Total	
				Survival
				Optional
				Culture
				Extra

Weekly Spending

	Monday _____	Tuesday _____	Wednesday _____	Thursday _____
Survival (food, medicine, transport, children, etc.)				
Optional (bars, restaurants, takeaway, shopping, etc.)				
Culture (books, music, shows, movies, magazines, education)				
Extra (irregular things such as gifts, repairs, furniture, unexpected expenses etc.)				

Month: _____   Week 5

Friday _____	Saturday _____	Sunday _____	Total	
				Survival
				Optional
				Culture
				Extra

Review of the Month

Your spending by category

	Survival	Optional	Culture	Extra
Week 1				
Week 2				
Week 3				
Week 4				
Week 5				
Total				

Your savings this month

Your total outgoings for the month:	
How much did you have to spend? ❶ - ❷	
How much did you decide to save?	
How much did you actually save?	

Did you achieve your goal for savings? ☐ Yes ☐ No ☐ So close

Month:

Reflections on the month in seven words or less:

If only...

What will you do to improve next month?

Your Plan for the Month

Income for the Month
(projected salary, rental income, royalties, benefits, pension, etc.)

Date	Source	Amount	Date	Source	Amount
Date	Source	Amount	Date	Source	Amount
Date	Source	Amount			

Total Income: ❶

Regular Monthly Outgoings

Rent or Mortgage		Car Insurance			
Utilities (Gas, Electric, Water)		Health Insurance			
Phone		Other Insurance			
Internet		Credit Card Payments			
Cable		Loan Payments			
Memberships		Parking			
Home & Contents Insurance		Commuting (train, bus, petrol...)			
Life Insurance					

Total Outgoings: ❷

Money available: ❶ - ❷

Month:

How much into savings this month?

Your goals for the month:

Your promises to make sure you achieve your goals:

Weekly Spending

	Monday _____	Tuesday _____	Wednesday _____	Thursday _____
Survival (food, medicine, transport, children, etc.)				
Optional (bars, restaurants, takeaway, shopping, etc.)				
Culture (books, music, shows, movies, magazines, education)				
Extra (irregular things such as gifts, repairs, furniture, unexpected expenses etc.)				

Month: [   ]   **Week 1**

Friday _____	Saturday _____	Sunday _____	**Total**	
				Survival
				Optional
				Culture
				Extra

Weekly Spending

	Monday _____	Tuesday _____	Wednesday _____	Thursday _____
Survival (food, medicine, transport, children, etc.)				
Optional (bars, restaurants, takeaway, shopping, etc.)				
Culture (books, music, shows, movies, magazines, education)				
Extra (irregular things such as gifts, repairs, furniture, unexpected expenses etc.)				

Month: _____   **Week 2**

Friday _____	Saturday _____	Sunday _____	Total	
				Survival
				Optional
				Culture
				Extra

Weekly Spending

	Monday _____	Tuesday _____	Wednesday _____	Thursday _____
Survival (food, medicine, transport, children, etc.)				
Optional (bars, restaurants, takeaway, shopping, etc.)				
Culture (books, music, shows, movies, magazines, education)				
Extra (irregular things such as gifts, repairs, furniture, unexpected expenses etc.)				

Month: [   ]   Week 3

Friday _____	Saturday _____	Sunday _____	Total	
				Survival
				Optional
				Culture
				Extra

Weekly Spending

	Monday _____	Tuesday _____	Wednesday _____	Thursday _____
Survival (food, medicine, transport, children, etc.)				
Optional (bars, restaurants, takeaway, shopping, etc.)				
Culture (books, music, shows, movies, magazines, education)				
Extra (irregular things such as gifts, repairs, furniture, unexpected expenses etc.)				

Month:

Week 4

Friday _____	Saturday _____	Sunday _____	Total	
				Survival
				Optional
				Culture
				Extra

Weekly Spending

	Monday _____	Tuesday _____	Wednesday _____	Thursday _____
Survival (food, medicine, transport, children, etc.)				
Optional (bars, restaurants, takeaway, shopping, etc.)				
Culture (books, music, shows, movies, magazines, education)				
Extra (irregular things such as gifts, repairs, furniture, unexpected expenses etc.)				

Month: _____ Week 5

Friday _____	Saturday _____	Sunday _____	Total	
				Survival
				Optional
				Culture
				Extra

Review of the Month

Your spending by category

	Survival	Optional	Culture	Extra
Week 1				
Week 2				
Week 3				
Week 4				
Week 5				
Total				

Your savings this month

Your total outgoings for the month:	
How much did you have to spend? ❶ - ❷	
How much did you decide to save?	
How much did you actually save?	
Did you achieve your goal for savings?	☐ Yes ☐ No ☐ So close

154

Month:

Reflections on the month in seven words or less:

If only...

What will you do to improve next month?

Your Plan for the Month

Income for the Month
(projected salary, rental income, royalties, benefits, pension, etc.)

Date	Source	Amount	Date	Source	Amount
Date	Source	Amount	Date	Source	Amount
Date	Source	Amount			

Total Income: ❶

Regular Monthly Outgoings

Rent or Mortgage		Car Insurance	
Utilities (Gas, Electric, Water)		Health Insurance	
Phone		Other Insurance	
Internet		Credit Card Payments	
Cable		Loan Payments	
Memberships		Parking	
Home & Contents Insurance		Commuting (train, bus, petrol...)	
Life Insurance			

Total Outgoings: ❷

Money available: ❶ - ❷

Month:

How much into savings this month?

Your goals for the month:

Your promises to make sure you achieve your goals:

Weekly Spending

	Monday _____	Tuesday _____	Wednesday _____	Thursday _____
Survival (food, medicine, transport, children, etc.)				
Optional (bars, restaurants, takeaway, shopping, etc.)				
Culture (books, music, shows, movies, magazines, education)				
Extra (irregular things such as gifts, repairs, furniture, unexpected expenses etc.)				

Month: [ ] Week 1

Friday _____	Saturday _____	Sunday _____	Total	
				Survival
				Optional
				Culture
				Extra

Weekly Spending

	Monday _____	Tuesday _____	Wednesday _____	Thursday _____
Survival (food, medicine, transport, children, etc.)				
Optional (bars, restaurants, takeaway, shopping, etc.)				
Culture (books, music, shows, movies, magazines, education)				
Extra (irregular things such as gifts, repairs, furniture, unexpected expenses etc.)				

Month: _____ **Week 2**

Friday _____	Saturday _____	Sunday _____	Total	
				Survival
				Optional
				Culture
				Extra

Weekly Spending

	Monday _____	Tuesday _____	Wednesday _____	Thursday _____
Survival (food, medicine, transport, children, etc.)				
Optional (bars, restaurants, takeaway, shopping, etc.)				
Culture (books, music, shows, movies, magazines, education)				
Extra (irregular things such as gifts, repairs, furniture, unexpected expenses etc.)				

Month:

Week 3

Friday _____	Saturday _____	Sunday _____	Total	
				Survival
				Optional
				Culture
				Extra

Weekly Spending

	Monday	Tuesday	Wednesday	Thursday
Survival (food, medicine, transport, children, etc.)				
Optional (bars, restaurants, takeaway, shopping, etc.)				
Culture (books, music, shows, movies, magazines, education)				
Extra (irregular things such as gifts, repairs, furniture, unexpected expenses etc.)				

Month: ☐   Week 4

Friday ____	Saturday ____	Sunday ____	Total
			Survival
			Optional
			Culture
			Extra

Weekly Spending

	Monday _____	Tuesday _____	Wednesday _____	Thursday _____
Survival (food, medicine, transport, children, etc.)				
Optional (bars, restaurants, takeaway, shopping, etc.)				
Culture (books, music, shows, movies, magazines, education)				
Extra (irregular things such as gifts, repairs, furniture, unexpected expenses etc.)				

Month: ⬜ Week 5

Friday ____	Saturday ____	Sunday ____	Total	
				Survival
				Optional
				Culture
				Extra

Review of the Month

Your spending by category

	Survival	Optional	Culture	Extra
Week 1				
Week 2				
Week 3				
Week 4				
Week 5				
Total				

Your savings this month

Your total outgoings for the month:	
How much did you have to spend? ❶ - ❷	
How much did you decide to save?	
How much did you actually save?	

Did you achieve your goal for savings? ☐ Yes ☐ No ☐ So close

Month:

Reflections on the month in seven words or less:

If only...

What will you do to improve next month?

Your Plan for the Month

Income for the Month
(projected salary, rental income, royalties, benefits, pension, etc.)

Date	Source	Amount	Date	Source	Amount
Date	Source	Amount	Date	Source	Amount
Date	Source	Amount	**Total Income:** ❶		

Regular Monthly Outgoings

Rent or Mortgage		Car Insurance			
Utilities (Gas, Electric, Water)		Health Insurance			
Phone		Other Insurance			
Internet		Credit Card Payments			
Cable		Loan Payments			
Memberships		Parking			
Home & Contents Insurance		Commuting (train, bus, petrol...)			
Life Insurance		**Total Outgoings:** ❷			

Money available: ❶ - ❷

Month:

How much into savings this month?

Your goals for the month:

Your promises to make sure you achieve your goals:

Weekly Spending

	Monday _____	Tuesday _____	Wednesday _____	Thursday _____
Survival (food, medicine, transport, children, etc.)				
Optional (bars, restaurants, takeaway, shopping, etc.)				
Culture (books, music, shows, movies, magazines, education)				
Extra (irregular things such as gifts, repairs, furniture, unexpected expenses etc.)				

Month: _____			**Week 1**	
Friday _____	Saturday _____	Sunday _____	**Total**	
				Survival
				Optional
				Culture
				Extra

Weekly Spending

	Monday _____	Tuesday _____	Wednesday _____	Thursday _____
Survival (food, medicine, transport, children, etc.)				
Optional (bars, restaurants, takeaway, shopping, etc.)				
Culture (books, music, shows, movies, magazines, education)				
Extra (irregular things such as gifts, repairs, furniture, unexpected expenses etc.)				

Month: _____   Week 2

Friday _____	Saturday _____	Sunday _____	Total	
				Survival
				Optional
				Culture
				Extra

Weekly Spending

	Monday _____	Tuesday _____	Wednesday _____	Thursday _____
Survival (food, medicine, transport, children, etc.)				
Optional (bars, restaurants, takeaway, shopping, etc.)				
Culture (books, music, shows, movies, magazines, education)				
Extra (irregular things such as gifts, repairs, furniture, unexpected expenses etc.)				

Month: [ ] Week 3

Friday _____	Saturday _____	Sunday _____	Total	
				Survival
				Optional
				Culture
				Extra

Weekly Spending

	Monday	Tuesday	Wednesday	Thursday
Survival (food, medicine, transport, children, etc.)				
Optional (bars, restaurants, takeaway, shopping, etc.)				
Culture (books, music, shows, movies, magazines, education)				
Extra (irregular things such as gifts, repairs, furniture, unexpected expenses etc.)				

Month: _____   **Week 4**

Friday _____	Saturday _____	Sunday _____	**Total**	
				Survival
				Optional
				Culture
				Extra

Weekly Spending

	Monday _____	Tuesday _____	Wednesday _____	Thursday _____
Survival (food, medicine, transport, children, etc.)				
Optional (bars, restaurants, takeaway, shopping, etc.)				
Culture (books, music, shows, movies, magazines, education)				
Extra (irregular things such as gifts, repairs, furniture, unexpected expenses etc.)				

Month: [   ]   **Week 5**

Friday ___	Saturday ___	Sunday ___	Total	
				Survival
				Optional
				Culture
				Extra

Review of the Month

Your spending by category

	Survival	Optional	Culture	Extra
Week 1				
Week 2				
Week 3				
Week 4				
Week 5				
Total				

Your savings this month

Your total outgoings for the month:	
How much did you have to spend? ❶ − ❷	
How much did you decide to save?	
How much did you actually save?	

Did you achieve your goal for savings?   ☐ Yes   ☐ No   ☐ So close

Month:

Reflections on the month in seven words or less:

If only...

What will you do to improve next month?

Annual Review

Your spending by category

	Survival	Optional	Culture	Extra
Month				
Month				
Month				
Month				
Month				
Month				
Month				
Month				
Month				
Month				
Month				
Month				
Total				
%				

Reflections on the year in seven words or less:

If only...

What will you do to improve next year?

© Spicy Journals 2018

Printed in Great Britain
by Amazon